Mandrills

Written by
Ruth Daly

www.av2books.com

MEDIA ENHANCED BOOKS
AV²
BY WEIGL™
ADDED VALUE • AUDIO VISUAL

Go to **www.av2books.com**, and enter this book's unique code.

BOOK CODE

A998247

AV² by Weigl brings you media enhanced books that support active learning.

AV² provides enriched content that supplements and complements this book. Weigl's AV² books strive to create inspired learning and engage young minds in a total learning experience.

Your AV² Media Enhanced books come alive with...

Audio
Listen to sections of the book read aloud.

Video
Watch informative video clips.

Embedded Weblinks
Gain additional information for research.

Try This!
Complete activities and hands-on experiments.

Key Words
Study vocabulary, and complete a matching word activity.

Quizzes
Test your knowledge.

Slide Show
View images and captions, and prepare a presentation.

... and much, much more!

Published by AV² by Weigl
350 5th Avenue, 59th Floor
New York, NY 10118
Websites: www.av2books.com   www.weigl.com

Library of Congress Cataloging-in-Publication Data

Daly, Ruth.
Mandrills / Ruth Daly.
     pages cm. -- (Amazing primates)
 Includes index.
ISBN 978-1-4896-2882-4 (hardcover : alk. paper) -- ISBN 978-1-4896-2883-1 (softcover : alk. paper) --
ISBN 978-1-4896-2884-8 (single user ebk.) -- ISBN 978-1-4896-2885-5 (multi user ebk.)
1. Mandrills--Juvenile literature. I. Title.
 QL737.P93D27 2014
 599.8'6--dc23
                                    2014038984

Printed in the United States of America in Brainerd, Minnesota
1 2 3 4 5 6 7 8 9 0 18 17 16 15 14

122014
WEP081214

Project Coordinator: Katie Gillespie
Art Director: Terry Paulhus

Photo Credits
Weigl acknowledges Getty Images, iStock, Minden Pictures, and Alamy as its primary photo suppliers for this title.

Contents

Meet the Mandrill

Mandrills are **mammals**. They belong to the **order** of **primates**. Mandrills are the largest **species** of monkey. They have tails, though very short ones. Male mandrills are very colorful. Their faces and hindquarters are bright blue, crimson, and pink. Female mandrills are less colorful than the males.

Mandrills live in groups known as troops, which have one male as leader. About 40 to 50 mandrills make up a troop. Sometimes, troops join together to form one large group, called a horde. The largest horde ever found was made up of 1,300 mandrills in Lopé National Park, Africa. Hordes are very noisy because mandrills communicate with each other using loud grunts and screams.

Mandrills are shy
and tend to stay
away from humans.

All About Mandrills

Monkeys are divided into Old World and New World monkeys. Old World monkeys come from Africa, India, or Asia. New World Monkeys come from Mexico, Central America, or South America. Mandrills are Old World monkeys and are only found in Africa. They live in the forests of Cameroon, Gabon, Equatorial Guinea, and Congo.

There are 133 species of Old World monkeys including macaques and baboons. Mandrills are often confused with baboons because they look similar to one another. One difference is that baboons have long tails and mandrills do not.

Mandrills are diurnal. This means that they are active during the day and rest at night. Like many other primates, mandrills like to spend time grooming each other.

Male mandrills are much bigger than females and weigh twice as much.

Comparing Primates

Because there are so many species of primates, scientists split them into subgroups. Each of these subgroups is called a superfamily. There are six superfamilies of primates. Grouping primates makes it easier to study their similarities and differences.

Lemurs

+ **Length:**
3.5 to 28 inches
(9 to 71.1 centimeters)
excluding tail
+ **Weight:**
1.1 ounces to 21
pounds (30 g
to 9.5 kilograms)
+ **Special Feature:**
Lemurs are the primate
at the highest risk
of **extinction**.

Tarsiers

+ **Length:**
3.6 to 6.4 inches
(9.1 to 16.2 cm)
excluding tail
+ **Weight:**
2.8 to 5.8 ounces
(79.3 to 164.4 g)
+ **Special Feature:**
Tarsiers have
the largest eyes,
compared to body
size, of all mammals.

Lorises

+ **Length:**
7.5 to 15 inches
(19 to 38 cm)
+ **Weight:**
9 ounces to 4.6 pounds
(255 g to 2 kg)
+ **Special Feature:**
Lorises are the only
poisonous primate.
They secrete a **toxic**
oil from a gland in
their elbow.

Old World Monkeys

+ **Length:**
13.4 to 37 inches
(34 to 94 cm)
excluding tail
+ **Weight:**
25 ounces to
110 pounds
(700 g to 50 kg)
+ **Special Feature:**
They have nostrils
that are narrow and
point downward.

New World Monkeys

+ **Length:**
5.5 to 28 inches
(14 to 70 cm)
excluding tail
+ **Weight:**
4.2 ounces to
33 pounds
(120 g to 15 kg)
+ **Special Feature:**
They have nostrils
that are broad
and point outward.

Apes

+ **Length:**
3 to 6 feet
(90 cm to 1.8 meters)
+ **Weight:**
12 to 399 pounds
(5 to 181 kg)
+ **Special Feature:**
Apes do not have tails.
They are the most
intelligent of
all primates.

Mandrill History

The family line of the mandrill goes back millions of years to the **Miocene** era. The earliest **ancestor** in the mandrill family was a large primate from the **genus** Parapapio. It lived in eastern and southern Africa.

Parapapio lived partly on the ground. It ate fruit and made its home in woodland areas. This is similar to how mandrills live today. Mandrills, drills, mangabeys, and baboons are all linked to this ancestor.

Over millions of years, each species developed differently. Mandrills do not have the curved fingers and long tails that are needed for swinging through the trees the way some monkeys, such as spider monkeys, do. When mandrills travel through trees, they use their limbs instead.

LINKS TO THE PAST

Traces of the mandrill's ancestors have been found that date back 5 million years.

Brighter colored males have a better chance of finding a mate.

Where Mandrills Live

Mandrills mainly live in **tropical rainforests**. They can also be found in coastal forests and **savannas**. Mandrills are terrestrial. This means they spend most of their time on the ground.

The area where mandrills live and search for food is called their territory. Mandrills have a special scent on their bodies that they rub on tree bark. They do this to mark their territory so that other animals will stay away. Their territory can be as large as 19 square miles (49 square kilometers), and they will defend it from rivals. Mandrills can travel about 6 miles (9.6 km) in one day.

WIDE RANGE

Mandrills have a larger territory than most other forest primates.

Female mandrills have a close bond to their mothers for most of their lives.

Mandrill Features

The bodies of mandrills have special **adaptations** that help them travel in trees, as well as on the ground. With their long limbs and strong bodies, they can climb and move from one tree to another by leaping sideways. They spend most of the day looking for food on the ground, but sleep in trees at night to stay safe from **predators**.

5

4

Getting Closer

① Cheeks

- Large cheek pouches that extend down the neck
- Can store almost a stomach-load of food

② Canine Teeth

- 2.5 inches (5 cm) in length
- Used in self-defence
- Baring teeth can be a friendly gesture or greeting

③ Fingers

- Five fingers, including a thumb, on the hands and feet
- Fingernails instead of claws
- Thumbs are useful when climbing trees

④ Limbs

- Long forelimbs
- Knuckles on forelimbs aid walking
- Walk flat-footed on back feet

⑤ Coat

- Bright colors of male's coat attract females
- Bright colors fade with loss of status
- Coat gets brighter with excitement

What Do Mandrills Eat?

Mandrills eat many kinds of food. They like eating several types of grass, roots, fruits, fungi, and tree bark. As well as plants, they also eat eggs, worms, insects, lizards, and other small animals. Animals that eat both plants and animals are called omnivores.

Mandrills have strong forearms. These are useful when **foraging** for food. Mandrills can rip open logs, dig out roots, and crack open hard objects, such as nuts.

If they are in danger, mandrills can quickly stuff food into pouches in their cheeks. This frees up their hands to run away on all fours. When they want to eat the food later on, they push it into their mouths using the back of their hands.

FEEDING TIME

Mandrills spend more than half their time feeding.

Mandrills use their fingers and thumb to collect, prepare, and eat food.

Mandrill
Life Cycle

Mandrills will often mate between June and October. Babies are born about six months later. Females give birth to one baby at a time. It is rare for mandrill twins to be born. Females care for their young until they give birth again. This takes at least two years. Then, the young mandrills must start taking care of themselves.

Birth to **2** Weeks

Babies are born with their eyes open. They have pink skin and black fur. They weigh 1 to 2 pounds (0.5 to 0.9 kg). Baby mandrills cling to their mother's belly.

Female mandrills like to play, chat in groups, and groom each other. Mandrills use gestures and various sounds to communicate. When they slap the ground, they are showing aggression. When they shake their head and shoulders, they are asking to be groomed.

2 Years and Older

Young mandrills are fully **weaned** by about two years of age. Females mature at about three years of age. They stay living together in their troops. Males mature at about six years of age. Bright fur grows on their face and hindquarters. They leave their troops to live alone. They do not mate until about nine years of age. Mandrills can live for approximately 30 years in nature.

2 Weeks to 2 Years

As the baby gains weight, it travels on its mother's back. After two months, it begins losing its baby fur and grows an adult coat. The mother shows the young mandrill what foods to eat.

Conservation of Mandrills

The main predators of the mandrill are eagles, snakes, and leopards. However, they rarely **prey** on adult mandrills. Humans are a much bigger threat to the mandrill population. Mandrills are often considered to be pests, since they eat people's crops. Sometimes, this results in mandrills being illegally hunted, or poached.

Another major threat to the mandrill population is deforestation, or clearing of large areas of forest. People cut down trees to build houses, graze cattle, and farm. All of these activities are destroying the mandrill's **habitat**.

Lopé National Park is a conservation area in Gabon, Africa. Here, mandrills are safe from poaching. However, mandrills are still at risk of becoming **endangered**. Conservation groups, such as the World Wildlife Fund, are working hard to protect mandrills and their habitat.

KEEPING TRACK

Scientists tag mandrills to help find out how many are left in nature.

Logging sites break up mandrill populations.

Myths and Legends

In African folk tales, mandrills can play different roles. In some tales, they are wicked characters. In others, they are shy or secretive characters. Mandrills can also be symbols of beauty and wisdom.

Mandrills are known as 'the Devil of the Fang' because of their fierce expression and sharp teeth. They were given this name by the Fang people of Gabon, Africa. Even though they look fierce, mandrills are actually shy animals.

Often, mandrills are confused with baboons. In the movie *The Lion King,* the shaman Rafiki is described as a baboon because he has a long tail. However, the colored markings on Rafiki's face show that he is really a mandrill.

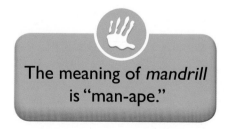

The meaning of *mandrill* is "man-ape."

Foraging Like Mandrills

Mandrills eat slippery foods, such as worms, and tiny foods, such as seeds. They catch fast moving animals, such as frogs and rats. Mandrills also dig in soil, sort through leaves, and rip bark to find food. For all of these foraging activities, mandrills have to be good with their hands. Test your foraging skills with the following activity.

Materials Needed: a tray, a small bucket, soil, leaves, twigs

List A: cooked pasta, leaves, pumpkin seeds, mushrooms, nuts, gummy worms, a small toy animal such as a plastic snake

List B: chopsticks, a clothespin, tweezers, a fork, a spatula, barbecue tongs

 STEP 1 Bury the items from List A in a shallow tray filled with soil. Cover the items with twigs and leaves.

 STEP 2 Now, try picking up the items buried in the soil using the items in List B. Try to move the buried items to the empty bucket without dropping them.

 STEP 3 Next, bury all the List A items again. Now, try picking them up and moving them to the bucket with your fingers and thumb. Is it easier to use your fingers and thumb or the items in List B?

5 Know Your FACTS

Test your knowledge of mandrills.

1 Mandrills are found in which African countries?

2 When are diurnal animals active?

3 When are the mandrill's fingers and thumbs particularly useful?

4 What are some of the ways that female mandrills socialize?

5 What are the main threats to mandrills in nature?

Key Words

adaptations: adjustments to the natural environment

ancestor: a relative that lived long ago

endangered: at serious risk of no longer living any place on Earth

extinction: no longer living any place on Earth

foraging: searching for food

genus: a level of classification above species

habitat: the environment in which an animal lives

mammals: warm-blooded live-born animals that drink milk from their mother

Miocene: a span of time in the history of Earth from 5.3 to 23 million years ago

order: in biology, a level of classification

poisonous: able to produce a harmful substance to protect itself from prey

predators: animals that hunt other animals

prey: to hunt other animals

primates: mammals with relatively large brains, flexible hands and feet, and good eyesight

rainforests: dense forests with heavy rainfall

savannas: grassy plains with few trees

species: animals that share many features and can produce offspring together

toxic: harmful substance produced by an animal or plant

tropical: a hot, wet climate

weaned: to have moved from drinking milk to eating food

Index

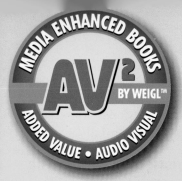

Log on to www.av2books.com

AV² by Weigl brings you media enhanced books that support active learning. Go to www.av2books.com, and enter the special code found on page 2 of this book. You will gain access to enriched and enhanced content that supplements and complements this book. Content includes video, audio, weblinks, quizzes, a slide show, and activities.

AV² Online Navigation

Book Pages
AV² pages directly correspond to pages in the book.

Key Words
Study vocabulary, and complete a matching word activity.

Quizzes
Test your knowledge.

Slide Show
View images and captions, and prepare a presentation.

Audio
Listen to sections of the book read aloud.

Video
Watch informative video clips.

Embedded Weblinks
Gain additional information for research.

Try This!
Complete activities and hands-on experiments.

AV² was built to bridge the gap between print and digital. We encourage you to tell us what you like and what you want to see in the future.

Sign up to be an AV² Ambassador at www.av2books.com/ambassador.

Due to the dynamic nature of the Internet, some of the URLs and activities provided as part of AV² by Weigl may have changed or ceased to exist. AV² by Weigl accepts no responsibility for any such changes. All media enhanced books are regularly monitored to update addresses and sites in a timely manner. Contact AV² by Weigl at 1-866-649-3445 or av2books@weigl.com with any questions, comments, or feedback.